"I Can Draw"
CARTOONS

Illustrated by Len Epstein

Hi! I'm Tippy the Pencil! I'm going to help you use this book. Whenever you see me, I'll give you hints on how to improve your drawing or have more fun.

Walter Foster

Here's what you need...

You're about to become an artist! Before you start, make sure you have a pencil, a pencil sharpener, an eraser, a felt-tip pen, and one or more of the different coloring media pictured here. Then, look in the back of the book for your grid pages. They'll help you to follow the special drawing steps. If you need more paper, you can ask a grownup to help you to copy them.

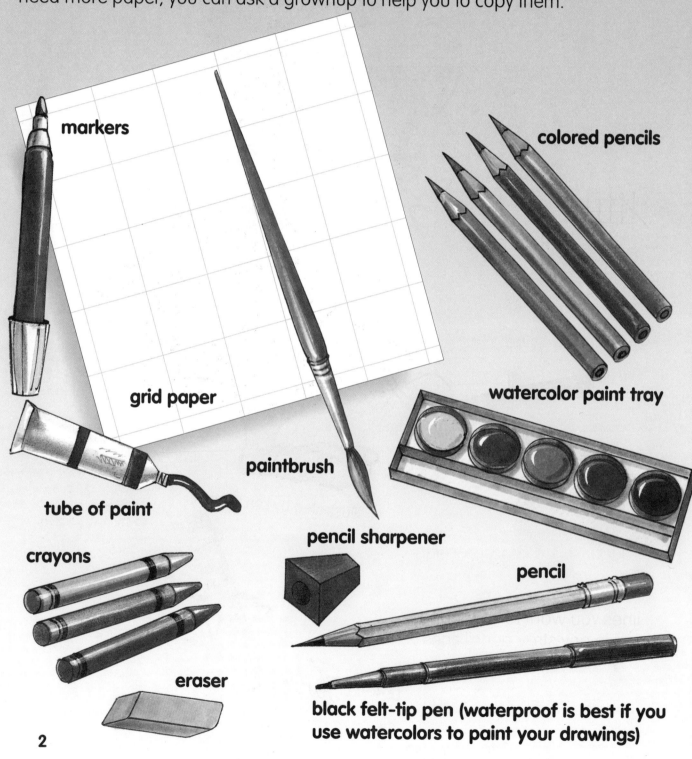

markers

colored pencils

grid paper

watercolor paint tray

tube of paint

paintbrush

pencil sharpener

crayons

pencil

eraser

black felt-tip pen (waterproof is best if you use watercolors to paint your drawings)

2

And here's what you do!

1 Copy each step-by-step drawing onto your grid paper, noticing where the drawing should touch the lines on your grid. Draw lightly in pencil. Since each new step is shown in blue, you'll always know exactly what to do next.

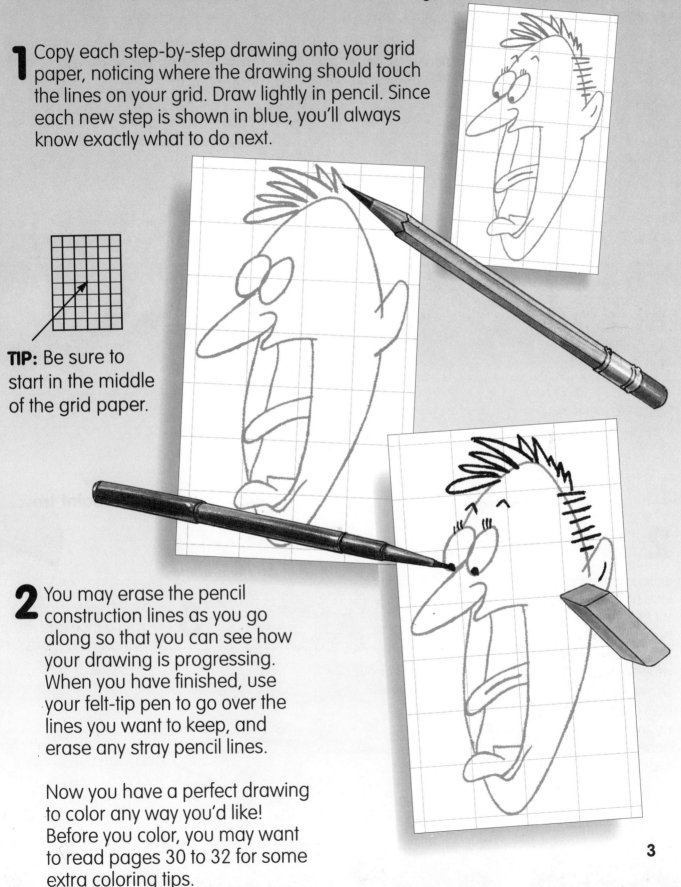

TIP: Be sure to start in the middle of the grid paper.

2 You may erase the pencil construction lines as you go along so that you can see how your drawing is progressing. When you have finished, use your felt-tip pen to go over the lines you want to keep, and erase any stray pencil lines.

Now you have a perfect drawing to color any way you'd like! Before you color, you may want to read pages 30 to 32 for some extra coloring tips.

The Good Guys

Everyone knows who the good guys are. They stand tall, have broad shoulders — and often wear capes!

Draw a long, curved line along which the main part of the figure will be positioned. This is called the "line of action". Start drawing the head, body, and legs.

1

2

Use rounded shapes for the arms and hands, and curved lines to draw the muscles on the chest. Draw the other leg and add the cape, a helmet, goggles, a nose, and details on the costume.

3

Finish your drawing with a face and hands, and more costume details.

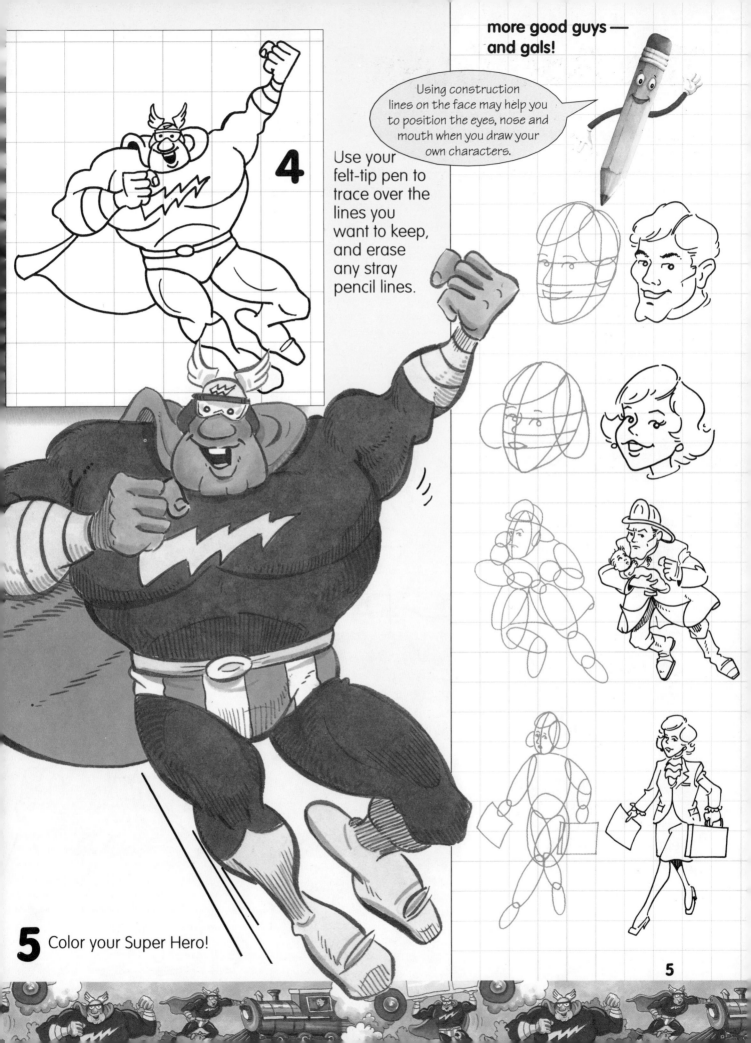

4 Use your felt-tip pen to trace over the lines you want to keep, and erase any stray pencil lines.

more good guys — and gals!

Using construction lines on the face may help you to position the eyes, nose and mouth when you draw your own characters.

5 Color your Super Hero!

The Bad Guys

Some of the most fun cartoon characters to draw are the bad guys. Whether you draw a wizened, evil scientist or a hulking bully, keep in mind that even the most sinister character can be funny, too.

Draw the scientist's lab jacket, pants, shoes, hands, hair, and facial features. Don't forget his test tube!

Draw the line of action. Use circles, ovals, and other round shapes to construct the head, body, arms, and legs.

Finish your drawing with eye pupils, glasses, eyebrows, a tie, and other details. Show smoke swirling over the scientist's head.

Use your felt-tip pen to trace over the lines you want to keep, and erase any stray pencil lines.

Special effects, like the smoke from the scientist's test tube, add drama to your drawing. Learn to draw more effects on page 24.

more bad guys

5 Color your Mad Scientist!

Funny Faces

In real life, expressions can be subtle and fleeting. Cartoons are not so subtle. Expressions are drawn at their most extreme — jaws drop in surprise, eyebrows turn down in anger, and mouths curl in sneers. Practice making faces in the mirror. Then copy your own expressions and exaggerate them until you achieve the effect you want.

1 Draw a long oval for the face, with another smaller oval inside it for the mouth. Add a carrot shape on one side for the nose.

2 Finish your drawing with hair, bulging eyes, an ear, and a wide-open mouth.

3 Use your felt-tip pen to trace over the lines you want to keep, and erase any stray pencil lines.

more expressions

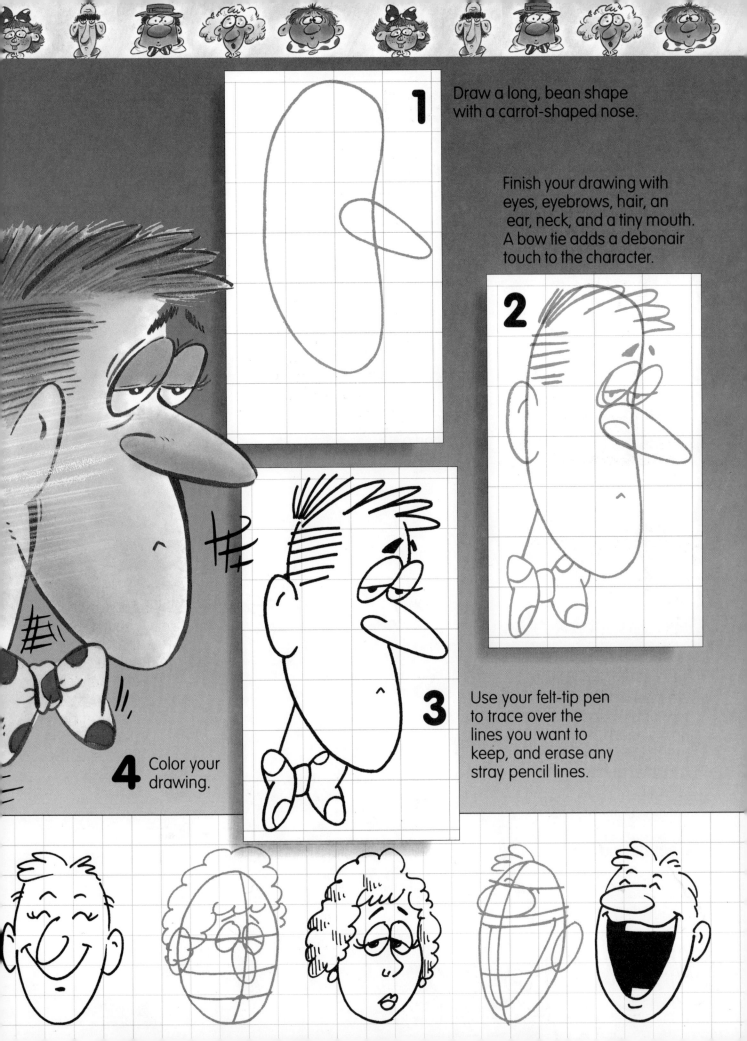

1 Draw a long, bean shape with a carrot-shaped nose.

Finish your drawing with eyes, eyebrows, hair, an ear, neck, and a tiny mouth. A bow tie adds a debonair touch to the character.

2

3 Use your felt-tip pen to trace over the lines you want to keep, and erase any stray pencil lines.

4 Color your drawing.

Hands & Feet

It's important to complete your cartoon character by giving it the right hands and feet. Hands and feet should be active — dancing, waving, kicking — even pulling a rabbit from a hat!

Start with the line of action. Draw the rabbit's body and his left arm and leg by using ovals and bean shapes. Add an oval on top for his ears.

Define the ears and the left arm and leg, and add the right arm and leg. Draw the rabbit's mouth and the fur on his head. Draw the magician's hands and put a top hat under the rabbit.

Finish the facial features and add fur on the chest. Define the right arm and leg and add detail to the top hat and the magician's sleeve. Draw the rest of the magician's fingers.

more hands and feet

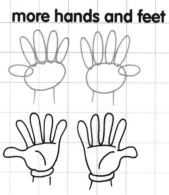

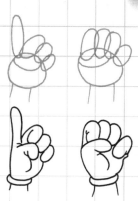

Notice how the magician has five fingers on each hand, but the rabbit has only four!

4

Use your felt-tip pen to trace over the lines you want to keep, and erase any stray pencil lines.

5 Color your drawing!

Animating Your Cartoons

Making your cartoons move is an art called animation. The movements necessary to complete an action are drawn in a series of steps.

A walk is one of the most common movements. Show your character lifting one foot as he puts the other down.

A storyboard is used to show the key points of an animated story. Here the action is drawn in a series of boxes.

Here, a simple sneeze is more fully animated.

Dressing Up

Your cartoon character's identity and personality
can be revealed in how he or she is dressed.
Notice how the rock musician and violinist on these
pages are drawn from the same basic form (Step 1).

Draw the line of action.
Build the head, body,
and legs with ovals and
rounded shapes.

1

Add the face and
hair, arms, jewelry,
and guitar body,
and define the
legs and shirt.

2

4 Color your
drawing!

Finish the guitar and the
hands and arms, and
add a necklace. Use your
felt-tip pen to trace over the
lines you want to keep.

3

2 Add the face, arms, and violin body, and define the clothing.

Finish your drawing and use your felt-tip pen to trace over the lines you want to keep.

3

4 Color your drawing!

Cartoon Caricatures

A caricature is a playful exaggeration of a realistic drawing. Caricature artists usually focus on the subject's most prominent feature and distort its proportions to an extreme. Compare the drawings shown here, and apply what you've learned to make your own caricatures.

Give the chef arms and hands, facial features, and clothing. Draw the dog's legs, ears, eyes, a nose, and tail. Add the string of sausages in his mouth.

1

Draw the lines of action. Use simple, rounded shapes to build the basic body forms.

2

Finish your drawing with details such as links in the sausages, a collar, pupils, feet, and fur on the dog, and eyebrows, a mouth, fingers, and details on the chef's clothing.

3

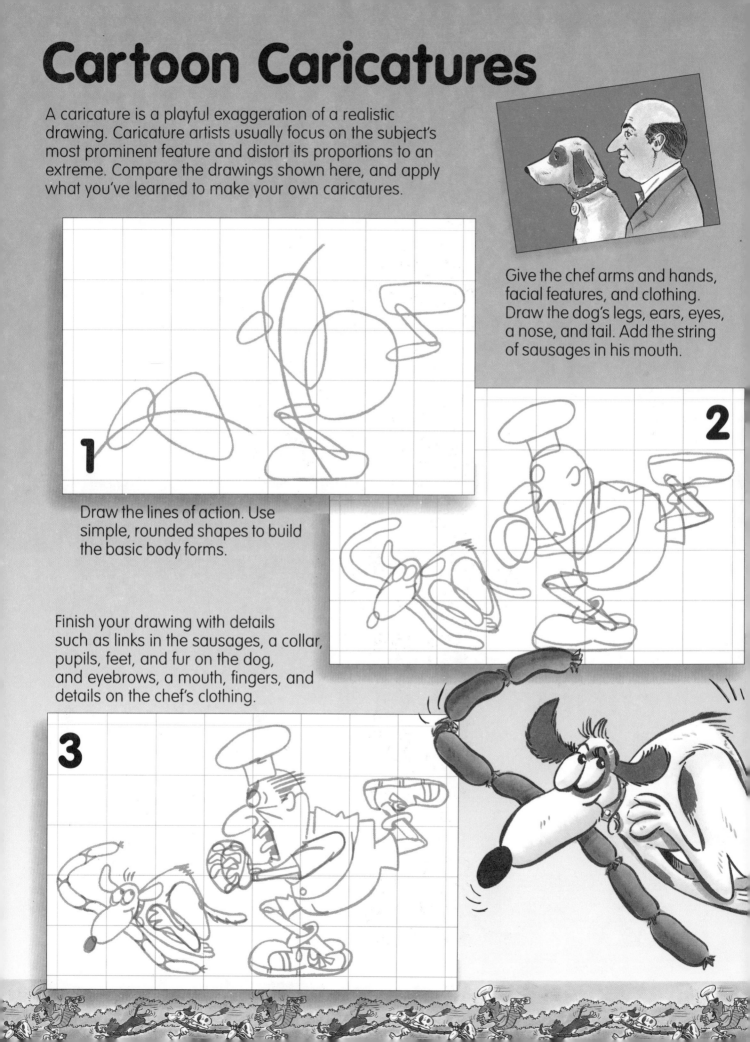

4

Use your felt-tip pen to trace over the lines you want to keep, and erase any stray pencil lines.

5 Color your caricature!

castle

flying saucer

circus tent

Making Backgrounds

Your cartoon characters can live in a town just like yours, or in their own world. Distorted proportions in the surroundings can add humor to the situation. In some ways, the background becomes another character in your drawing. Try drawing some of the backgrounds shown here, and then make up some of your own!

Learn to draw the dragon on page 28. ▲

Learn to draw the rabbit on page 10. ▲

Learn to draw the Super Hero on page 4. ▲

Learn to draw the clown on page 20. ▲

Learn to draw the Mad Scientist on page 6. ▲

Getting a Laugh

There's more to drawing a cartoon than just following some steps. Bring your sense of humor to the drawing board and put it into your pictures. The more absurd you make your cartoon character, the bigger the laugh will be.

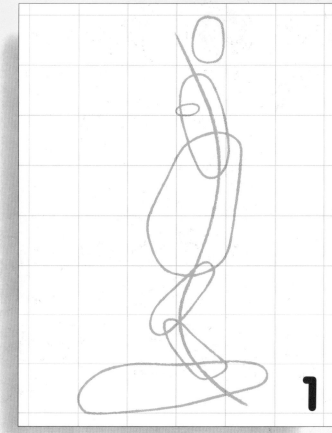

1

Draw the line of action, and build the basic form of the figure around it with simple shapes.

2

Add the arms, another leg, the face, suspenders, and part of the hat. Define the shape of the left leg and shoe.

Complete the face and add a bow tie, hands, and a squirting flower. Put the finishing touches to the costume.

3

4 Use your felt-tip pen to trace over the lines you want to keep, and erase any stray pencil lines.

5 Color your drawing!

more laughs

Robot Fun

High-tech science fiction characters offer the cartoon artist a chance to really go wild at the drawing board. There's no limit to the nuts, bolts, springs, wires, and other gizmos you can draw on your character. Think about the odd-shaped parts of a clock or a car engine, and experiment with them for heads, limbs, and bodies.

Draw the line of action. Use cubes, triangles, and other shapes to make up the cat robot's body. Use tiny shapes to make the mouse.

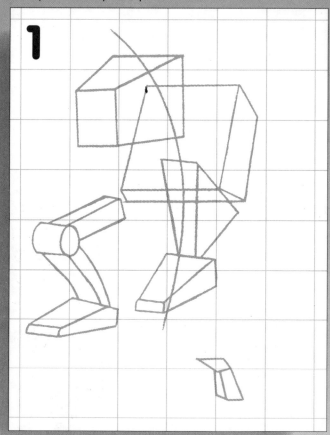

1

2

Draw the cat robot's arms. Give the mouse arms, legs, and a tail, and add the facial features and ears on each. Use circles and tubes for joints.

Finish your drawing by adding details such as pupils, whiskers, nuts and bolts, and seams.

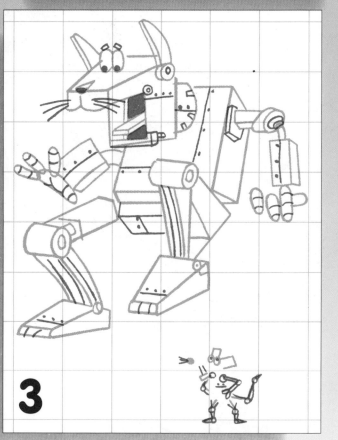

3

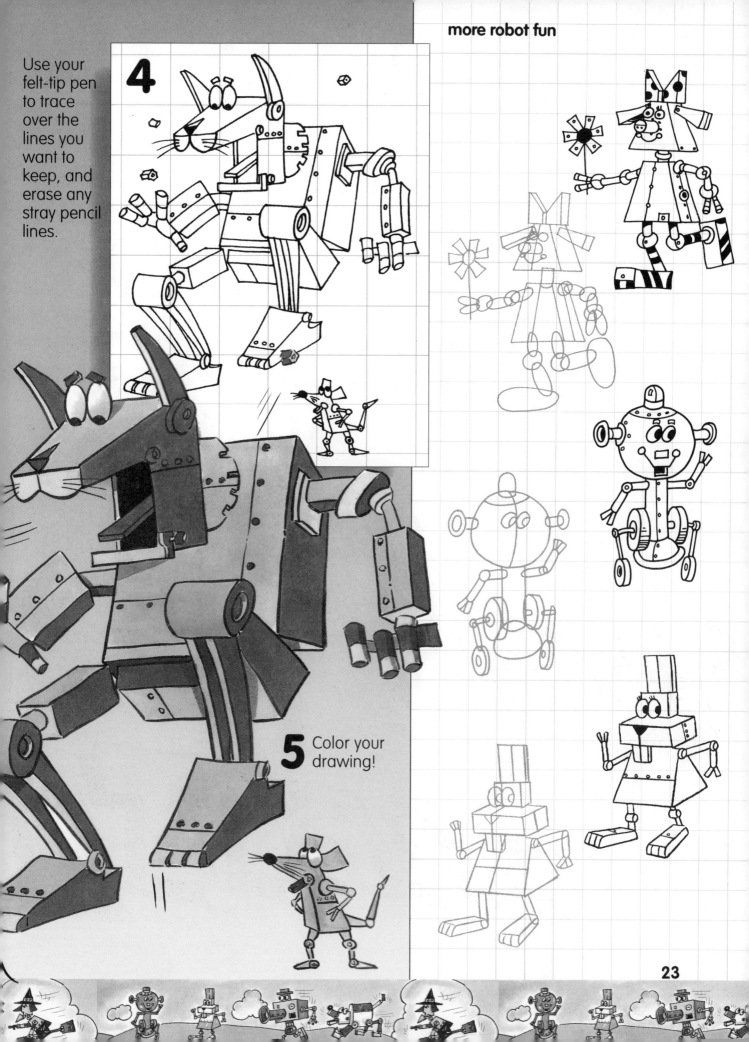

Use your felt-tip pen to trace over the lines you want to keep, and erase any stray pencil lines.

4

5 Color your drawing!

Special Effects

Special effects play an important part in making your cartoon funnier. Crashes, splats, zaps, and other sounds can be made part of your drawing by spelling the sound they make in large letters. Long "whoosh" lines follow the motion of a fast-moving object, and jagged lines show the point of impact. Whatever effect you want to achieve, remember to make it BIG!

AAAAAARRGGHH!

SLAM!!!

BONK

SPLATT

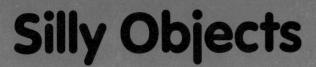

Silly Objects

It's possible to turn inanimate objects into cartoon characters with their very own personalities. The possibilities are endless — cars, trees, stars, and even ordinary household items come to life with the addition of a pair of eyes and a mouth. Try some of the cartoons shown here, and then let your imagination take over and try animating the objects around you!

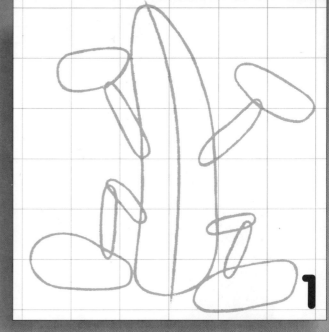

Start with the line of action. Draw the long, curved body and the hands and feet. Use thin oval shapes for arms and legs.

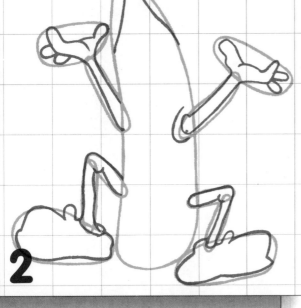

Give the top of the pencil a point and add definition to the hands, feet, arms, and legs.

Finish your drawing with a face, an eraser bottom, shoes, gloves and a lead tip.

more silly objects

26

Use your felt-tip pen to trace over the lines you want to keep, and erase any stray pencil lines.

4

5 Color Mr. Pencil!

27

Amazing Animals

Very often, cartoon artists choose to use animals instead of people in their drawings. Some animals are easily recognizable as certain character types. Bears and bulldogs are often bullies, a fox is sly, roosters are vain, and pigs are, well, pigs. Here's how you can use what you've learned already to humanize your animals.

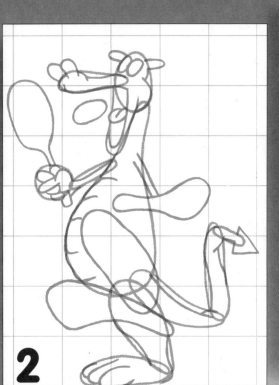

1 Draw the line of action. Use ovals, circles, and pear shapes to construct the basic form.

2 Add the face, and the left arm and leg. Define the body, and draw a point at the tip of the tail. Add a tennis racket and ball.

3 Finish your dragon with spikes down its back, teeth, nostrils, pupils, fingers, toes, and scales. Add broken strings and "whoosh" lines to the racket and ball.

4 Use your felt-tip pen to trace over the lines you want to keep, and erase any stray pencil lines.

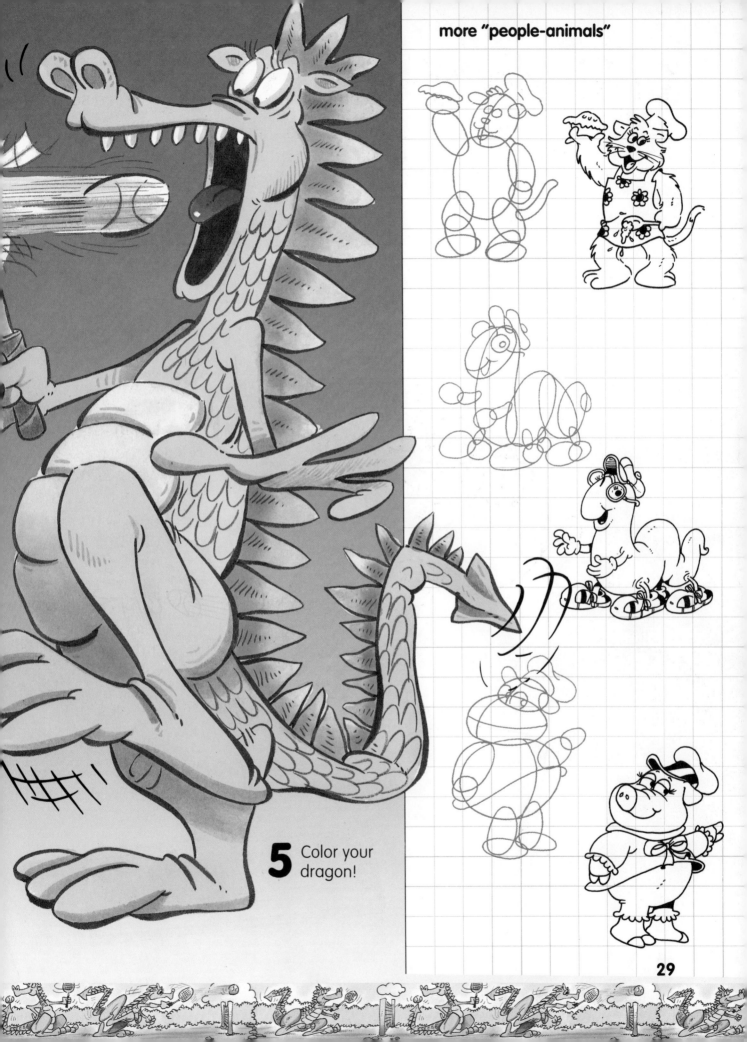

5 Color your dragon!

Coloring Your Drawings

Once you've finished the outlines of your drawings, it's fun to color them in. Use watercolor paints, colored pencils, crayons, markers, or anything else you can think of!

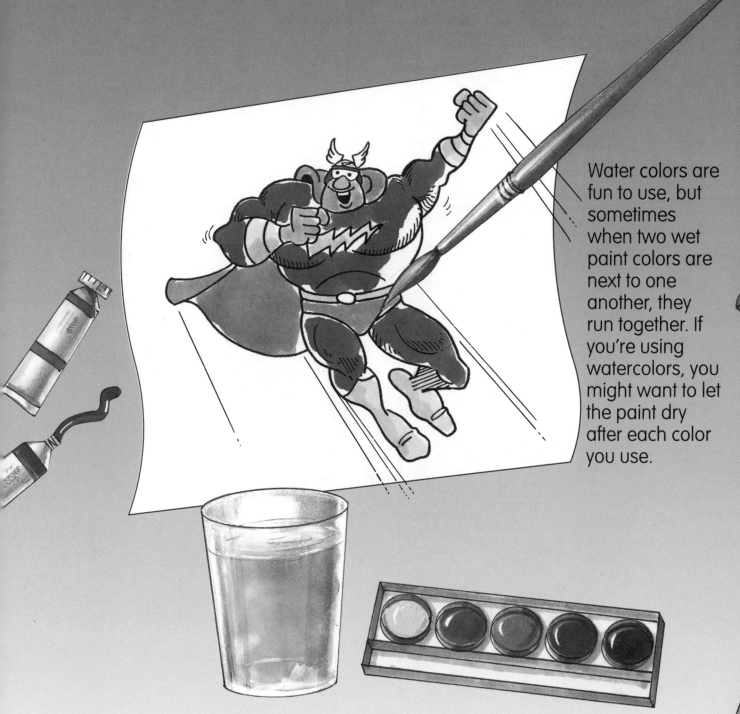

Water colors are fun to use, but sometimes when two wet paint colors are next to one another, they run together. If you're using watercolors, you might want to let the paint dry after each color you use.

Turn to the next page to learn a really special way to bring your drawings to life!

Markers give your drawings a smooth, bright finish and even colors.

Crayons and colored pencils are good for shading. See page 32 to learn how!

Shading Your Drawings

Shading can add dimension and life to your drawings. When coloring your cartoons, leave some areas lighter than others to show where the light would shine. Then try shading with a crayon or colored pencil and watch your drawing come to life!

Use these pull-out grid pages for your drawings. Make extra copies so you can draw lots of pictures using the steps in this book!

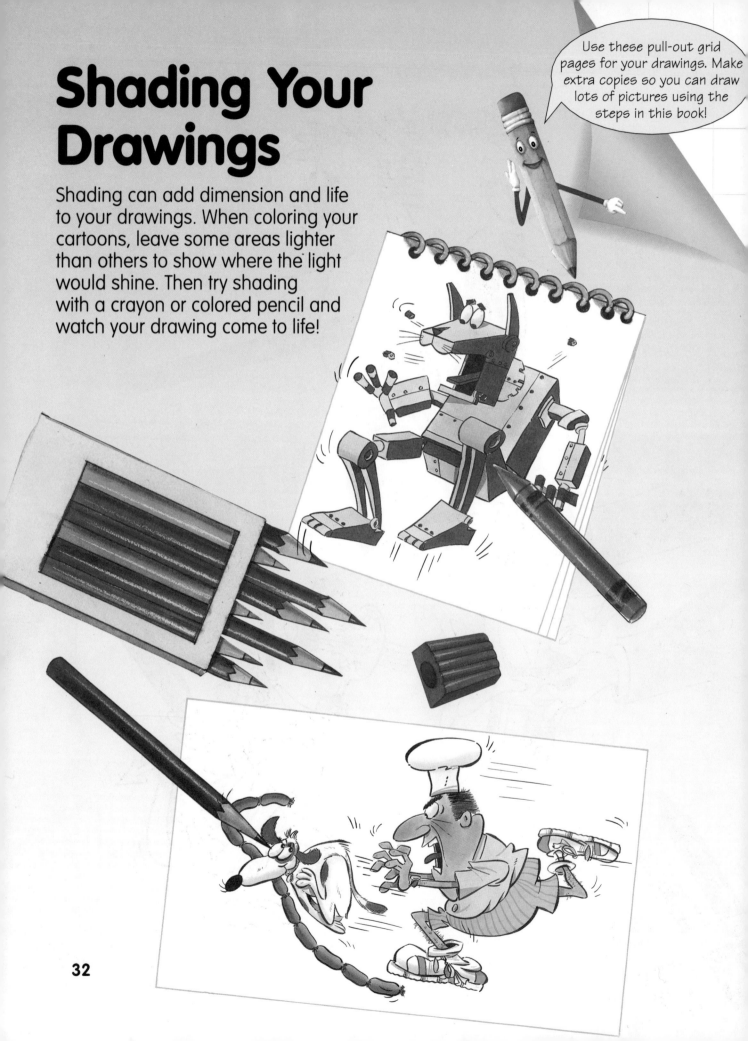